Weekly Reader Books Presents

SURVIVE!
...COULD YOU?

*By Judy Donnelly
and Sydelle Kramer*

Field Publications
Middletown, Connecticut

Dedication

To Amy and Sarah,
our most helpful critics.

ACKNOWLEDGMENTS

Many experts in the fields of disaster and wilderness survival were very helpful in the preparation of this manuscript. The authors are particularly grateful to the members of the New York, San Francisco, and Cincinnati chapters of the American Red Cross; the U.S. Guard, the New York City Fire Department, the Joshua Tree National Monument; and the American Museum of Natural History. We would especially like to thank Maris Cakors, Wayne Campbell, Ken Curtin, Lt. Cmdr. K. E. Fisher, Margo Hall, Lt. Robert Henesey, Siena Lindemann, Dan McClanahan, Bob Moon, Cheto Olais, Nancy Shade, and Sue Smith for their time and interest.

Contents

INTRODUCTION

Buried in an avalanche ...
Threatened by a tornado ...
Swept away in a flood ...
Nobody wants to be caught up in a terrible disaster, but everybody wonders what it would be like. "How would I feel?" people ask. "Would I do the right thing? Or would I be too scared even to move?"

This book will help you imagine what it's like to face a real catastrophe. It lets you think about the choices you might be forced to make. Then it explains what decisions give you your best chance for survival.

Luckily, you probably won't ever have to know what to do. But just in case, it's important to remember that no two fires (or tornadoes or earthquakes) are ever quite the same. Should you encounter one, it probably won't happen the way it does in the situations described in this book. And a disaster in the pages of a book just can't equal the terror of the real thing.

That's why—should the unlikely happen—the most important advice to remember is to stay calm. Then you can think clearly and act wisely.

This is *not* a survival guide. If you're interested, there's much more information you can get about surviving disasters. In the library, you'll find entire books on fire safety, for example, or living through a shipwreck. Even more important, these books can tell you how to prevent problems and stay safe if, for example, you're going on a desert hike or a boating vacation.

In the meantime, settle down in a nice, safe spot and get ready to face some dangerous situations—shark attacks...sandstorms...a tidal wave. And if they're too scary and you want to escape—just close the book!

BURIED ALIVE

The mountain towers over you. It's so tall you can't believe there's anything on the other side. And the day is so bright, so gleaming, that the sun on the snow makes rainbows that dance before your eyes.

It's early spring and you're saying good-bye to winter by skiing down one last slope. The day before, it snowed, but now the weather's unusually warm. You're alone on the mountain. The world is quiet and still.

Slowly you glide to the fresh slope that beckons, the one that no one's skied before. When the wind comes up, the top snow swirls and starts to cover your skis. A plane in the distance makes a low roaring sound and when it passes, you take off. All you can hear is the wind's soft breath and the dull crunch of your skis on the icy surface.

Suddenly, behind you, there's a whistle, as if someone were calling a dog. Then there's a growl, as if that dog were right behind you. You look around to see if anything's there. Nothing. It's peaceful again, but only for an instant.

Crack! There's a sound like a shot being fired and you look again. What's going on? Then you see it.

Above you, a huge sheet of snow is beginning to slip and slide down the mountain. It's coming right toward you, faster and faster. A roar fills your ears, a great cloud of snow hides the light. Snow smacks your face; ice grabs at your ankles. It's an avalanche! You've got to do something. But what?

Should you:

A. Throw away your skis and your ski poles?
B. Try to outski the avalanche—get down the mountain as fast as you can?
C. Ski into the avalanche?

The experts say the best answer is A, throw away your skis and poles. You won't be able to ski faster than an avalanche unless you're very far ahead of it and near the bottom of the mountain. An avalanche moves with the speed of a hurricane and that means it's going 60 miles an hour or more! You won't be able to ski anyway because anything moving as fast as an avalanche will knock you right off your feet. An avalanche is so powerful it can uproot trees and toss houses into the air. The only time you should stay on your skis in the face of an avalanche is when you can reach the side of the slope before the avalanche reaches you. If you make it to the side, the avalanche will slide right past you.

There's another reason for getting rid of your skis and poles—so you can swim better!

When the avalanche reaches you, it will knock you over as it heads down the mountain. You'll find yourself totally buried by snow and ice. As long as it's moving, though, you'll be able to move, too, and the best way to do that in snow is to swim on your back. That's right—do the backstroke! Keep your head up and swim toward the side of the avalanche where the snow won't be as deep as the middle.

But what if the avalanche brings down trees and rocks and solid blocks of ice?

Then forget about swimming and roll up into a ball. That way you'll protect as much of your body as possible, as well as your head.

Here's an important fact that hardly anyone would consider. In order to learn it, you have to answer a question that's going to sound silly, but it's really not.

While you're swimming or rolling through the avalanche, do you keep your mouth open or do you keep it shut?

You keep your mouth shut. It doesn't matter if you normally breathe better with your mouth open. If you keep it open, it may fill up with snow. The snow will soon start to melt because of your body heat and you won't be able to swallow it all—your mouth will be stuffed. If the snow melts into your lungs, you might actually drown.

What do you do when the avalanche stops?

A. Lie very still and not use up any energy.

B. Scream, scream, and then scream some more.

C. Dig your way out.

D. None of the above.

The answer is D, none of the above. You can't wait until the avalanche stops to try to save your life. Avalanches may be made of light, powdery snow. But once an avalanche stops, the snow can freeze so hard it will be like concrete all around you. It can be so thick and tight you'll be unable to move and you might not be able to breathe. So here's what you do: You wait for the avalanche to slow down. Then, while it's actually still moving slowly, you start digging all around you. You have to make an airspace—a place where there's no snow, just air, so you can breathe. If you're having trouble digging, at least put your hands over your mouth and nose. That way your hands will keep the snow away from your face and leave you some air to breathe. A few years ago, a woman was buried in an avalanche at a ski resort. Because she had an airspace, she survived for five days, and then she was rescued.

The avalanche is finally over. Everything is quiet. You're OK. But you're buried in a lot of snow. Now what?

When a wave knocks you down, don't you tumble and roll over and over till you're not really sure which way is up? Well, the same thing happens with an avalanche, only the avalanche doesn't wash away into the sea, leaving you sitting on the beach in shallow water. So when you're there in the middle of all this snow and ice, before you do anything, you have to figure out which way is up!

How do you think you do that?

A. Wait a minute and see if blood starts rushing to your head as it does when you're upside down.

B. Stick your hand up in all directions and feel where the air is warmest.

C. Spit and try to determine which way your saliva falls, then dig in the opposite direction.

If you look around and can't spot any light coming from the surface, then spit, and when you determine which way your saliva falls, dig in the opposite direction. You won't be able to feel if you're upside down, and since the snow is packed so tightly, no warm air will be able to get through. But if you spit into the air, the natural force of gravity will make your saliva fall toward the ground. Once you know which way is down, you also know which way is up. The idea is to dig through to the surface or as close to it as possible. That way you can be rescued more quickly and more easily.

How are people buried in avalanches rescued?

The first thing that rescue patrols or people who are not caught in the avalanche look for is anything sticking out of the snow, like legs or arms. They listen for cries of help. Then they walk on top of the avalanche, taking care not to miss any spots, and poke their skis or ski poles through the snow to see it they hit anything with them. If they do, they dig up that spot. Official rescue teams often come up the mountain with dogs specially trained to sniff out buried people. Experienced skiers and mountain climbers sometimes wear what's called an avalanche cord—a brightly colored, very light rope—around their waists. If an avalanche occurs, they untie one end of the cord and hope it will stick up through the snow after the avalanche is over. Today, they're even more likely to carry a transceiver, which operates on battery power. If someone carrying a transceiver is buried in an avalanche, the rescuer can carry a matching unit that picks up the beep of the buried transceiver. Then the rescuer knows exactly where to dig.

What caused this avalanche anyway?

A. the wind
B. the warm weather
C. the snowfall the day before
D. the plane flying overhead
E. skiing down the slope
F. none of the above
G. all of the above

The correct answer is G, all of the above, since one of these by itself could have caused it, or all of them acting together.

Is there any way to avoid being caught in an avalanche?

Absolutely. If you happen to be in avalanche country—steep, bare mountains covered with snow—you can avoid being caught in an avalanche just by looking around you. Trees help hold snow on mountainsides. If you're skiing below or through trees, an avalanche is not likely to strike. On the other hand, a treeless strip on a mostly tree-covered mountain is a place where avalanches do happen. There are other warning signs. Don't ski on or below a slope that looks cracked. Keep from skiing below any area that has a great bulge of snow protruding from it. If you have to travel a suspicious-looking slope, ski up or down, not across it. Listen to weather reports and keep in mind that most avalanches occur within a day and a half of a snowstorm. And remember, most avalanches happen over and over again in exactly the same spots, so find out where those spots are and always avoid them.

In the story at the beginning of this chapter, you broke the first rule of avalanche country.

What's the most important rule to remember when you're on a high mountain covered with snow?

A. Never ski alone.

B. Never ski in warm weather.

C. Never ski down a fresh slope.

D. Never ski on a mountain over which planes fly.

The first rule of avalanche country is never ski alone. If you're with friends, chances are that not all of you will be swept up in the avalanche. That way, someone will be right there to rescue you immediately.

JAWS

The water is so warm and clear that you could float in it forever. Small fish the color of rainbows dart in and out of the waves.

The sun's in your eyes but you see something in the distance. It looks like a triangle pushed on its side. You blink, and now it's even closer.

"Shark!" you hear someone screaming. "Shark! Get out of the water!"

You head for shore, but you don't know if you can make it. The fin is behind you, swimming faster and faster.

What do you do?

A. Splash around and make a lot of noise.

B. Stay perfectly still.

C. Dive underwater.

D. Swim quietly, quickly, and smoothly toward the beach.

The correct answer is D, stay as calm as you can and swim quietly, quickly and smoothly to the beach. Don't try to move faster than you've ever moved before—that will make you jerk around. Splashing and very sudden movements in the water catch a shark's attention. You want to seem like an ordinary fish in the ocean. If the shark starts circling around you, avoid swimming in its direction.

What do you do if you can't get away from a shark?
A. Face it and stare into its eyes.
B. Put your head underwater and blow bubbles.
C. Hit it on its nose, its gill, or its eye.
D. All of the above.

No matter how scared you are and how much you just want to swim away as fast as you can if a shark turns up right next to you, do all of the above.

Turn and face the shark and make yourself look right at it. Some sharks are afraid of bubbles and loud noises, so sink underwater and blow air through your mouth. If you have something in your hand or if there's a large object floating in the water, use it to hit the shark on its nose. Don't use your hand because the skin of a shark is so rough it will cut you. Once there's blood in the water, the shark *won't* go away. If you can't reach its nose, try for its eye or its gill. A gill is where the shark breathes—there are five of them in a row on each side of the fish.

If there are a few of you in the water, make a circle with all of you facing out of the circle toward the shark. Sharks would rather attack a person swimming alone. That's one reason why experts advise you never to swim alone.

If you fall overboard don't take off your bathing suit or any other clothing you might be wearing. Your clothes will protect you from the shark's skin, and if it brushes past you, you won't bleed.

Sharks are so attracted to blood that experts warn against swimming in the ocean with a cut or wound that's still bleeding since sharks can smell blood a quarter of a mile away! Their senses are so keen that if you're not swimming smoothly, they can feel your jerky movements 100 feet away and they can hear you 1,000 yards away—that's almost two-thirds of a mile.

If you absolutely have to go into water that sharks may inhabit, do it only during the day. Then at least you'll be able to see the shark coming. In addition, there are more shark attacks at night since that's when they go hunting for food. Experts further believe that you should never swim in dirty water since you won't be able to see very well.

They also warn you not to wear bright colors—sharks are less attracted to dark colors, especially black.

What if you're in a raft or a boat and a shark gets close?

Keep everything you have inside the boat and try to stay quiet. The shark may just go away. If it doesn't, grab a paddle and hit it on the nose. Don't throw garbage overboard, particularly food with blood in it—you don't want a shark to think that by following your boat, it will get a great meal. If you catch a fish and a shark approaches, let go of the fish. You don't want to have a fight with a shark.

There's something else you can do. No matter what, it's always a good idea to keep shark repellent in your boat.

Since sharks don't like it, they go away when you throw it into the water.

Remember, though, when you go to the beach this summer—don't be afraid to go into the water. In the United States, you're more likely to get hit by lightning than be bitten by a shark.

THE GREEN SKY

You're walking down a quiet street at the edge of town. All around you the land stretches out flat as a ruler and you can see for miles and miles. It's been a hot, clear day, but the weather seems to be changing. There's a sickly green glow to the sky and black clouds are forming in the distance, like balloons hanging low on the horizon. It looks as if thunderstorms may be coming.

It starts to get dark, although sunset is hours away. The heavy clouds shove each other around in the sky. Soon there's just one cloud, as big as a giant, racing closer and closer, coming right toward you. You've never seen anything quite like it. There's a faint rumbling, like thunder growling, and it seems as if the cloud is eating up the sun. You can see part of the cloud turning one way while another glides in the opposite direction. It wobbles and spins like a slow-moving top.

You realize you're scared. You start to walk fast, but the wind holds you back: It's blowing so hard you have to shut your eyes. Suddenly you hear whistling, then hissing, in front of you, and when you open your eyes, something's hanging from the cloud. It's sliding and curling like a snake through the sky. It whirls and twirls toward you, whistling louder and louder.

You're breathing very hard and your heart is starting to pound. The giant cloud slides closer, and the thing hanging beneath it has changed from a snake to a dark gray ice-cream cone. The cone is spinning madly, getting darker and darker.

You know what it is now—a tornado, a twister! It's whirling right toward you.

What do you do?

A. Try and find shelter.

B. Run.

C. Dig a hole and bury yourself.

You should try and find shelter. When a tornado hits, there's nothing you can do but get out of the way. Not even the weather forecaster can tell what it's going to do or where it's going to go. Its path is completely unpredictable. When it spins round and round, it's twirling up to 500 miles per hour, but it's also moving forward or backward or side to side at an average speed of 40 miles per hour.

And then there's its size to consider. Some tornadoes are only 200 yards across (about two city blocks), but others are as wide as a mile. It would take you 20 minutes to walk across a mile-wide tornado, if you could!

Also, they're tall. The smallest ones are 800 feet high (imagine three city blocks sticking up in the air) and the tallest ones are half a mile high (that's the length of seven football fields placed end to end).

Tornadoes may last for just a few minutes or they can last as long as three hours. They're strong, they're powerful, and they're extremely frightening, but here's a comforting thought: If you're in the right shelter, 99 times out of 100, you'll be just fine.

So there you are in the middle of the street, the tornado spinning in front of you. The wind is screaming as it tears at your hair. Blue-green bolts of lightning color the sky, and you have to dodge debris as it whizzes past your head. You look around quickly.

Of all the places you see, which is the right shelter?
A. a tree house
B. a mobile home or trailer
C. a room with windows
D. the school gym or auditorium
E. a tennis court
F. none of the above

None of these is the right shelter.

You don't want to climb into a tree house since a tornado can easily uproot a tree. You and the tree and the house will go flying.

A mobile home or a trailer isn't like a regular house. It has no foundation so the winds of a tornado might blow it right across town.

Remember what happened to Dorothy just before she blew up to Oz? That's right, she was lying on her bed next to the window. Dorothy was silly. If a tornado is

16

nearby, never stay in a room with windows. And if you're stuck in one, don't lie down on the bed. Get under it. Take your pillows and your mattress and put them on top of you. You need as much protection from flying glass and falling chunks of ceiling as you can get.

If you're in school, don't go to the auditorium or the gym. The bigger the space, the weaker the roof and you don't want to be in a room whose roof just blew away, do you? Head for the bottom floor and stay in a hallway away from the windows.

You might be on the tennis court, or playing soccer on the lawn, or you could just be out for a stroll. It doesn't really matter where you are if you're outside because that's the worse place to be. But if you can't get inside when a tornado hits, look for a ditch or the lowest possible space and lie down flat on your stomach with your arms over your head. Your feet should be pointing toward the storm so your head gets the most protection from the wind. Don't lie down in a drain or any place where water collects. It can rain so hard in a tornado that such areas can flood.

OK, you know where *not* to go. But the tornado's moving fast. The wind is punching you around. First it rains, then it hails. It's as dark as midnight outside. You've got to take cover. But where?

For what kind of shelter should you look?

The best place is a special storm cellar.

In tornado country—mostly the Midwest and parts of the South—people build concrete shelters underground. Some build them toward the southwest corner of their homes because they think the wind will be less powerful there. The doors of the shelter always open inward so if a tree falls across them, they can still be opened. Emergency supplies are stored in the shelters: first-aid kits, blankets, flashlights, tools, and, of course, food and water, in case people have to be in the shelter for a while.

But suppose you don't see a storm cellar anywhere. The closest thing is a white frame house. You run toward it as fast as you can. You push the door open, grateful it wasn't locked. "Help!" you shout. No one answers. You're in a kitchen. Will you be safe here?

Where's the safest place to be in a house during a tornado?

A. the bathroom
B. the basement
C. a closet
D. a hallway

The safest place is the basement, but if there is none, a bathroom, a closet, or a hallway are pretty good second choices—anywhere that's in the middle of the first floor of the house. Don't stay upstairs—the higher you are, the stronger the wind will be.

The basement is the most safe since it's the lowest part of the house and usually below ground. Some people think you should stay in the part of the basement closest to the storm, but others think you should go to the corner opposite the wind. No one's really sure, since tornadoes are unpredictable, but everyone agrees the basement's the best place to be.

The bathroom, because it has pipes, is stronger than most other rooms. But if it has a window, it might not be safe. Instead go to a closet in the middle of the house. The rooms around it will help to protect it from the wind.

The same thing is true of a hallway in the middle of the house. If there's a heavy table around, you can get under that for added protection.

No matter what part of the house you choose, put your hands over your head and neck to protect them from anything the wind might blow your way.

You look around the kitchen. There are three closed doors. Does one lead to the basement? Through the kitchen window, you see the tornado racing toward you, knocking down trees, smashing trucks to bits. There's no time to lose! You throw open the nearest door. There are stairs leading down!

A few seconds later, you're huddled in the corner of the basement. There's a noise that sounds like 500 planes all taking off together. You hear shutters flapping and what sounds like glass breaking. Is the tornado about to rip open the house? You're so frightened you're breathing as if you had just run 20 miles.

Then suddenly it's quiet. The tornado whistles away. You lift your head slowly—now you can see. When you feel yourself all over, you realize you're OK. But you can't help wondering what's coming up next.

What do you do after a tornado?

It's better to ask what you *shouldn't* do.

Don't go near any power lines on the road that may have fallen down. You can get a bad electric shock.

Don't walk into any building that's been damaged by the storm. It may fall down while you're in it.

Don't light a match or lantern in a house unless you know the gas has been turned off. It's better to walk around in the dark than cause an explosion or a fire.

Don't let anybody smoke until you're sure there's no danger of fire or explosion.

You can't stop thinking about how lucky you were. You keep remembering how it felt when that tornado was coming right at you. You wonder...

What would happen if you were caught in the middle of tornado?

Many years ago some people were actually trapped in the middle of a tornado and survived. It's very unusual and may never happen again. Here's what they said: Like the eye of a hurricane, a tornado's center is still—the wind doesn't blow although the clouds around you are spinning. The noise is deafening, lots of screaming and hissing, and the air smells of gas. Your ears pop the way they do in a fast-moving elevator, and you might have trouble breathing because the air is so thin. You see the thick top of the tornado and the much thinner bottom. Lightning bounces from side to side.

What causes a tornado?

A. high winds
B. cold air meeting warm air in a special way
C. a cloud that explodes
D. none of the above

Answer B is correct. A tornado happens when cold air meets warm air in a particular way.

Warm air is wet; cold air is dry. When they bump into each other, the warm air usually rises above the cold air.

When a tornado forms, however, the cold air ends up on top. Then the warm air crashes into it, trying to rise, but the cold air pushes back and traps it. If there's a crack in the cold air, the warm air will shoot through it at 200 miles per hour. The cold air falls down. What you get is a huge thundercloud. All around the bottom, air pushes in, giving the rising warm air a twist. A twist, and a twist, and still another twist, and pretty soon the warm air is whirling. A tornado is the fastest, strongest wind ever felt on earth.

Because there's cold air left over from winter and warm air arriving for spring, there are more tornadoes between April and June than at any other time. The United States has more, 500 a year, than any country in the world, with the Midwest and the South getting hit by almost all of them. Tornadoes usually move from the southwest to the northeast. They frequently spin counterclockwise. Their lightning is blue-green, with up to 20 bolts a second!

In 1884, there were 60 tornadoes that hit three states in just one day. And in 1955, 6 twisters spun down to earth from the same cloud.

You know a tornado is strong. You know a tornado is wild. You know a tornado can break and smash exactly what it wants.

What else can a tornado do?

A. Suck the water from a well.
B. Move your refrigerator from the kitchen to the attic.
C. Remove the feathers from a chicken.
D. Blow a train from the tracks to a meadow.
E. Steal a blanket off a bed.

F. Carry two men down the street.

G. Lift an egg without breaking its shell.

H. None of the above.

I. All of the above.

At one time or another, tornadoes really have done all of the above. And the two men and the chicken didn't even get hurt!

Of course, not everyone's that lucky. Tornadoes, as you know, pick up whatever's in their way. They suck things in; they spit things out. The winds on the outside toss everything away, but the inside is very different. Unlike normal air, the air is so thin, that like a vacuum, it sucks in whatever it wants; if it sucks in a whole house, the house might explode.

Can a tornado ever occur on water?

Yes, it can, but when it does, it's called a waterspout.

Tornadoes over water aren't as strong as tornadoes over land, but they still can be a mile high. Full of water, hail, and ice, the wind will suck up even more water to make a huge fountain shooting into the sky. Sometimes fish and frogs and turtles—anything near the top of the water—will get sucked up in it, too. A waterspout is very loud; there's a lot of hissing and sighing and sucking, all at top volume.

The tornado's over now and you're safe. But you know it can happen again.

Is there a way to find out if a tornado's coming?

A. Keep a pair of binoculars in your house.

B. Set up a powerful telescope on the roof.

C. Listen to the weather report.

D. There's no way to find out.

Since the National Weather Service is always on the lookout for tornadoes, you can find out if one is coming just by listening to the weather report. Weather forecasters can't tell exactly where and when a tornado might hit, but they can figure out if a tornado is forming before it actually does. The Weather Service issues bulletins over radio and television called tornado watches and warnings. Always pay attention to a warning, since that means a tornado is probably on its way.

THE ONE-MINUTE ESCAPE

What a busy day you had today! The whole family stayed home cleaning and making repairs. Everyone worked hard, but there was no time to get tired. Dad fixed the hot-water heater (Mom said he'd never be able to do it.) Your sister stored everyone's old clothes in the attic. Mom rearranged the family room.

You helped them all. You carried Dad's gasoline can from one basement room to the other. You made a pile of all the dirty rags. You pointed out to Mom the torn lamp wire and the socket where all the plugs were falling out. In the attic, you nearly burned yourself on the bare light bulb hanging from the ceiling. That reminded you to tell your sister to turn it off when she was through.

At night, everyone took it easy. Dad built a fire that was still burning when he and Mom went to bed. He fell right to sleep, but Mom started smoking and reading a book.

Now you're tucked in yourself, and it's so warm and comfortable you think you'll stay in bed forever. You know you'll sleep well and dream pleasant dreams.

But just before dawn while it's still dark outside, you wake up with a start. Your mouth is very dry and you feel as if you have a fever. There's a strange smell in the room, and your eyes begin to sting. Your ears feel as if they're burning.

Your door is closed, but you can hear strange noises outside it—crackling and popping and the crash of something falling. Somewhere glass is breaking, pieces scattering on the floor. It's so dark in the room you feel as though you're blind, but when you turn on your lamp, there's just a click! Nothing happens.

You try to take a deep breath, but it only makes you cough. The air is heavy, as if a hand is on your mouth, sweat is pouring down your body like water from a shower. It's hot and smoky—could your house be on fire?

You throw off your blankets but lie still in bed. You're alone. You have to save yourself.

What do you do?

A. Jump out of bed, get your favorite things, then run out of the room.

B. Climb up on a piece of furniture and stand near the ceiling.

C. Crawl under your bed and wait for someone to come and help.

D. Go back to sleep and hope you're just dreaming.

E. None of the above.

Do absolutely none of the above. DON'T EVEN SIT UP IN BED! If you think your room may be full of

26

smoke, *roll* out of bed and onto the floor. Do it quickly, as fast as you've done anything in your life! Keep your head as close to the ground as you can. You'll be able to see better near the floor and you'll have more air to breathe. It will also be cooler.

In a fire, smoke and heat fill the top of a room first. No matter how scared you are, don't climb on any furniture. And don't stand up if the room is even a little smoky or hot. Smoke and heat hurt more people than fire itself. Smoke travels faster than flame and is full of a poison gas called carbon monoxide. If you start breathing carbon monoxide, you won't be able to get out of the room at all. Carbon monoxide can paralyze you and then choke you. Also, if a fire burns plastic, the smoke can be so poisonous that only two breaths may knock you out. Poison gas is often invisible, so even if there isn't much smoke, it may be harmful to breathe the air. That's why the best thing to do in a fire is always stay close to the floor.

The heat of a fire is also very dangerous. The temperature has to reach only 150 degrees to make a person faint, but fires give off a lot more heat than that. The ceiling of a room on fire can reach 600 to 700 degrees—so hot that a phone in the room next door will melt, so hot flames can suddenly burst out without even needing a spark. Just breathing in that kind of heat can melt your lungs and "glue" them together: One breath would be enough to kill you.

However, while the ceiling's burning, the temperature on the floor may be only 80 degrees. That's why the floor is where you must be. But that doesn't mean you should crawl under your bed and stay there. When there's a fire, you have to act quickly to save your life, so never stay in just one place hoping someone will come along to rescue you.

Flames could be outside your door. You can feel the room slowly filling with smoke. The wires downstairs must be burning; that would explain why your lamp won't turn on.

How much time do you have to get out of your house?
A. 1 minute
B. 2 minutes
C. 10 minutes
D. 20 minutes

You may have as little as one minute to get out of the house! Even if there aren't any flames on your floor or in your room, the fire may be raging downstairs. When a fire gets that hot, it doesn't just burn, it can explode! You don't want to be trapped.

So there you are flat on your stomach, lying on the floor. You're not going to stand up, even if there's not very much smoke above you. You can see better now than you did from your bed, and you're not feeling quite so warm.

Suddenly you realize you're wearing only your pajamas.

Should you get dressed before you try to get out of your house?
A. Wear whatever you have on, even if that's nothing.
B. Change into your best clothes so they don't get burned up in the fire.
C. Change into your worst clothes in case you get dirty.
   Don't stop for anything. Wear whatever you have on

and if you have nothing on leave anyway. You may have only a minute to get out of your house.

So you're on the floor in your pajamas. What next? *Where do you go now?*

A. Crawl over to the door.
B. Take a deep breath and run into your closet.
C. Get to a phone any way you can and call the fire department.

Never, never stand up—you know that. Crawl to the door of your room. That's right, *crawl*, like a baby. Don't get into your closet. You could be trapped by smoke and flames and not be able to get out. Forget about calling the fire department now. You have to get out of the house first.

Your bedroom door is closed. DON'T OPEN IT YET. First, feel all around it, even the doorknob. Is it hot? Is smoke floating in from the bottom or the sides?

If the door feels hot, don't even think about opening it. The temperature may be at least 200 degrees higher on the other side. Flames and thick smoke may be waiting to enter. A closed door always slows a fire down. It stops what's called a draft, the pull of cooler air on very hot air that makes the hot air travel faster. Fire follows a draft into open rooms, up and down staircases, out broken windows, through caved-in roofs.

But drafts can help fight fires, too. When fire fighters arrive at a burning building, they actually set out to *create* a draft. That's how they force a fire to travel the path they want. They make a hole in the roof or in the floor of the highest room of the house so the heat and smoke will rise and follow the draft right out. Then it gets cooler downstairs, and the fire fighters can enter the building. There's also more air for them to breathe.

When you touch the door, it feels hot. You know you mustn't open it even though that's what you really want to do. You have to think fast even though it seems as if you're moving in slow motion.

What do you do when the door is hot?

A. Stuff a towel or sheet or whatever you can reach under it to keep the smoke out.
B. Try not to breathe fast so your lungs don't quickly fill with smoke and gas.
C. Pound on the wall or the door to try to wake everyone else up.
D. Crawl to the window.
E. All of the above.

Do all of the above as quickly as you can and try shouting "Fire!" to make sure everyone is awake. But don't be surprised if your voice isn't very loud—smoke and heat and gas can make it very weak. If you have a whistle, try blowing it. Remember: You don't have much time, so don't spend more than few seconds stuffing the towel under the door and pounding on the walls. Then get to the window.

DON'T OPEN IT ALL THE WAY, just a crack. If you throw it wide open, an explosion could occur. Or a strong draft through the window might pull the fire right *through* your door.

Once the window is open a little bit, keep opening it slowly. If you're on the first floor, jump out as soon as there is enough space to climb through the window. If you're on the second, climb out on the sill and hang down, feet first. Then, when you let go, you fall the shortest distance possible. If you're higher and might hurt yourself if you jump, it's best to wait for help. If it really seems necessary, you can make a rope from sheets and blankets by knotting them together and tying them to something heavy. Climb onto the window sill and slide down the rope. It should be long enough to let you jump safely to the ground.

Jump only if you know you'll land safely.

What if you're too high up to jump and there's no way to get down?

A. Crawl back to the door.

B. Stay by the window.

C. Jump anyway.

Stay by the window. Leave it open about three inches at the top and three inches at the bottom. The smoke and heat will escape out the top and fresh air will come in through the bottom. If you can reach water, wet a towel or handkerchief and cover your mouth and nose. You'll breathe in less smoke and you'll also feel cooler. You can even wet a blanket and wrap it around yourself.

Don't forget to wave something out the window so that when the fire fighters arrive, they'll know you're there.

If you can't open the window, don't hesitate—*break it.* Grab anything heavy and hammer through the glass. Even if you can't jump out, the window should be open to let gas and smoke escape and fresh air enter.

Let's backtrack a little. Imagine you've crawled over to your bedroom door and it's *cool* to the touch. What then?

What if the door isn't hot?

A. Slowly open it and run out.

B. Go to the nearest phone and call the fire department.

C. Stay by the bedroom window anyway.

If the door feels cool, you should try to open it, but do it *very, very slowly.* Remember: You can't be sure what's on the other side. Flames can rush in before you have time even to yell "Fire!" The heat may be strong enough actually to knock you down. Lean forward against the door and be ready to shut it quickly. Take a deep breath and open it just a crack. If it seems as though the world's strongest man is on the other side, close it tightly. If nothing pushes back, open it a little more. If there's not much smoke and it's not too hot, go out. Shout "Fire!" to waken everyone. Head for the outside. Whatever doors you open, close behind you.

Suppose you encounter flames and thick smoke on the way out?

If fire or thick smoke blocks your way and you can't go on, head for the roof. Don't stop to try to fight the fire and don't worry about the fire department. Just get out!

You made it! You're outside now with the rest of the family. Your neighbors must have called the fire department because the engines are right in front of your house. People from up and down the block come over to make sure everyone's all right. You stand there and watch the flames attack your bedroom. Water starts pouring from the longest hoses you've ever seen, and a fire fighter comes over to say things will be under control in a matter of minutes.

Your house will be damaged, but it will be saved. Your escape, however, could have been easier and a little less scary.

What's missing from this story that all families should have to make sure no one gets hurt in a fire?

A. smoke detectors

B. flashlights

C. an escape plan

D. all of the above

You and your family should have all of the above.

Smoke detectors sound an alarm as soon as smoke reaches them. There should be at least one on each floor of your house or apartment. Smoke detectors make such a loud, high-pitched noise that no one could possibly sleep through it. That's very important, since thousands of people die each year in fires simply because they don't wake up in time.

If you sleep with a flashlight next to your bed, you can grab it when you roll onto the floor. A flashlight will help you see, lighting your way to safety even if the room is smoky.

If you've already talked about and *practiced* an escape plan, you'll know exactly what to do. You'll know what to do if the fire's still small enough for all family members to get out together. You'll know what to do if the fire's so big you have to escape alone. No time is wasted thinking about what should come next.

Despite what you and your family didn't do to make sure no one gets hurt in a fire, there is something very important you *did* do.

What was the one thing you did before you woke up that helped to save your life?

A. Got a good night's sleep.
B. Closed your door.
C. Tried to turn on your lamp.
D. Threw off your blankets.

You remembered to close your door. Experts say that everyone should sleep with the door shut. Even a wooden door can hold back the hottest flames for about 15 minutes. A metal door can keep a fire out for nearly two hours.

Now you know what to do in case of a fire in a house. But what if you're in another kind of building?

What if there's a fire in a big hotel or a tall apartment building?

A. Run down the stairs and out of the building.
B. Get into the elevator and ride to the roof.
C. Stay in the hallway and wait for help.
D. Do almost the same thing you'd do in a house.

Pretend the door to the hotel room or the apartment is the door to your room at home, and then do just about the same thing you'd do in your house. Of course, if there's a fire escape, get down it as fast as you can.

Go to the main door and see if it's hot. If there's smoke in the air, remember to crawl. Don't open the door if it is hot, stuff towels underneath it.

Now you do something a little bit different. Go to the bathroom and fill the tub with water. Soak some towels and blankets and wet your clothes, too. Take everything with you to the room *farthest* from the main door. On your way there, *close all doors and windows behind you.*

Once you're in that room, close its door, too, but open the window. You'll probably be too high up to jump, but keep your head near the window and breathe in fresh air. At the same time, wave something for the fire fighters to see.

If your door *isn't* hot, go into the hallway. In a hotel or apartment building, there's almost always a staircase marked "Fire Exit" with a red sign. It's usually behind a closed door. But if the staircase is smoky, go back to the room or apartment.

Whatever you do, don't get into the elevator. You can be trapped there by the smoke and flames.

While you're trying to escape, something you're wearing may accidentally catch on fire.

What do you do if your clothes catch on fire?

A. Run for your life.

B. Fall on the ground and start rolling around.

C. Look for water.

Fall on the ground and start rolling around on whatever part of your clothing is burning. The flames will die out because you're cutting off the air supply they need in order to burn. If there's a blanket nearby, wrap yourself up in it and then roll around. The flames will die even more quickly.

As hard as this may be, *don't run*, whatever you do. Running just makes the flames burn faster.

Now you know how to escape a fire no matter where you are. Did you know there are 33 million fires in the United States each year? That's a fire a second! Lightning and very dry or hot weather cause a lot of them, but at least half are started accidentally by people. There are at least 300 different ways you can start a fire in your house without realizing it, so it's easy to see how such things can happen. Fires kill or injure more children each year than any other kind of accident, but you can learn how to keep that from happening to you.

Remember the beginning of this story?

What did you and your family do that could have started the fire?

A. Dad tried to fix the hot-water heater.
B. You left a gasoline can in the basement.
C. You made a pile of dirty rags.
D. There was a torn lamp wire.
E. There was a socket full of plugs falling out.
F. There was a bare light bulb in the attic.
G. Your parents left the fire burning after everyone went to bed.
H. Mom smoked in bed.
I. None of the above.
J. All of the above.

Any one of these situations could have caused the fire, so the answer is J, all of the above.

Only a real repair person should fix anything like a furnace or a hot-water heater, since such things might explode and start a fire. Also, no one but a trained electrician should fix anything electrical in your house. Remind your parents of this.

Never keep gasoline in the house. One can of gasoline explodes with the power of six sticks of dynamite!

Don't pile dirty rags together that may have chemicals on them, even rags your family uses for cleaning purposes. You can never tell how chemicals will react if they happen to get near something hot.

Never use anything electrical that has a torn wire—one spark can burn your house down. And never put too many plugs into one socket—making one outlet send out more power than it should can cause a fire.

There should never be a bare light bulb in a closet, a basement, or an attic. It may come into contact with something that will burn. When a light bulb's turned on, it can get really hot, and if it's close to clothing or paper, it can start a fire.

Always put out a fire in your fireplace completely— never leave it burning. Even after it's out, keep a screen around it until the ashes are completely cooled. That way you'll be sure no sparks can jump out.

Don't let anyone you know smoke in bed. If someone falls asleep and the cigarette is still lit, sheets and blankets can start burning from falling ash.

There are other things you can do to make your house safe from fire:

1. Don't play with matches, no matter how safe you think it is.
2. Don't play with cigarette lighters.
3. When a match is thrown away, make sure it's completely out.
4. Don't leave an electric heater or blanket on unless someone is in the room to watch it.

There is one last thing you should know. You may be sitting in the kitchen waiting for your dinner, watching your mom or dad cook something greasy like French

37

fries. Suddenly the pan catches on fire.

What should you do to put out a grease fire?

A. Put the pan in the sink and fill it with water.

B. Leave the pan on the stove and throw water on it.

C. Be patient and let the grease in the pan burn up.

D. Throw baking soda on the flames.

If something's burning on the stove or in the oven, the only way to put it out is by throwing baking soda on the flames. That's right—baking soda. Not flour, that can explode. Not water, it might explode, too. A grease fire is like a chemical fire or a gasoline fire—don't try to put it out with anything that may cause a reaction. Of course, if there's a fire extinguisher nearby, you can use that.

You also can't use water to put out a fire in a plug, or wire, or anything electrical. Since water conducts electricity, you could give yourself a terrible shock by throwing it on an electrical fire. Turn the power off: Either pull the plug, or if that's too hot, pull the fuse out of the fuse box or turn off the circuit breaker.

However if there's smoke coming out of your television set, *don't* pull the plug. Just turn the TV off and stay away from the picture tube. Picture tubes can explode. Don't turn the set on again until it's been repaired.

STUCK!

Stay calm. You can't *really* be sinking. There's no quicksand in these woods. You've been walking through this bog ever since you were little. Nothing like this could ever happen to you.

Then why is the mud sucking at your ankles? Why is the sand reaching up for your knees? Why do you feel as if you were stuck in a giant bowl of porridge? Horrible scenes from the movies flash through your mind. Will you slowly slip under and disappear?

Can you figure out what to do?

A. Swim for your life.
B. Stand absolutely still.
C. Pull your feet out by jumping up and down.
D. None of the above.

If you get stuck in quicksand, do none of the above.

Fall flat on your back with your face up, as if you were floating. Put your arms out to your sides. If people are

nearby, just lie there and wait for them to throw you something. You might be able to pull yourself out that way. If you're alone, roll slowly—that's right, *roll slowly* with careful movements over to firm ground. Move as smoothly as you can—don't struggle or push or pull because that could make you sink. You want the quicksand to have time, after each move you make, to flow back around your arms and your legs, just like water. It may take you an hour to roll your way out, but you'll be safe. If you're carrying anything with you, such as a knapsack on your back, drop it immediately. Don't hold onto anything that can weigh you down.

What if you're not really stuck yet?

A. Try to run out of it.
B. Try to wade out of it.
C. Try to reach for a tree branch to pull yourself out.
D. All of the above.

All of the above is the correct answer.

If you haven't sunk very far down into quicksand, say, only up to your ankles, you can try running or wading out of it. You just might escape before the quicksand has time really to grab you. But if you feel yourself sinking, stop and get on your back. Whatever you do, don't just stand there: the sand will turn to liquid under your feet and you will sink.

No matter how deeply you find yourself stuck in quicksand, if there's a branch overhead, you can try to pull yourself to safety. Do it slowly and carefully. Don't jump up and down trying to reach the branch or you'll sink.

How long does it take before quicksand covers you completely?

A. five minutes
B. an hour
C. a day
D. hardly ever

It's almost impossible for anyone to get covered up completely by quicksand. People usually don't sink beyond the waist. The water and the sand that make up quicksand are heavier than you are. But if you're really stuck and you can't get out, you could starve to death before someone finds you.

Quicksand occurs when there's so much water in the sand it's no longer strong enough to hold you up. The sand isn't packed together as it is at the beach. Each grain rests upon a cushion of water, not on other grains of sand. When you step on sand in a desert, a swamp, a bog, or at a river's mouth, you sink.

SURF'S UP!

You're at the beach with a surfboard; the sun is shining; there's a nice, warm breeze. You're all set to dash into the ocean when you hear your parents calling, "Get off the beach! Hurry! There's a big wave coming! A tidal wave!"

A big wave, you think—*that's great! Why should I leave!* But your parents are in no mood for an argument. You get going and before you know it, you're not just off the beach, you're on top of a mountain! Your mother and father say it's the safest place to be. You're starting to ask yourself, "Just how big is this wave anyway?"

From the mountain, you can see the ocean below. It's starting to look strange: The water seems to be running out of the harbor. It's all sand and mud where just minutes ago ocean used to be. Suddenly in the distance, a giant wave appears. It's getting taller and taller. It's the biggest wave you've ever seen, as tall as a building!

You hold your breath. The wall of water towers over the beach. It's as though the entire ocean has gathered in one incredible wave.

Now you know why you're not down on the shore. If you'd stayed there, you might have drowned.

How did your parents know a tidal wave was coming?
A. They saw it long before you did.
B. They heard a Coast Guard warning.
C. They measured the height of the waves at the beach.

The U.S. Coast Guard has a tidal wave warning system, so your mom and dad probably heard that one was coming just by listening to the radio. Even if they didn't hear the warning on the radio, the Coast Guard makes sure that everyone in the danger zone is told to leave. The Coast Guard can even tell you approximately when the wave will arrive.

The west coast of the United States is studied more carefully than the east coast since it's much more likely to be hit by a tidal wave. That's because earthquakes cause tidal waves and the west coast has more of those.

You didn't feel an earthquake. You're sure you wouldn't have missed one.

How far does an earthquake have to happen from where you live to cause a tidal wave right near your house?
A. It can happen a mile away.
B. It can happen 100 miles away.
C. It can happen 1,000 miles away.
D. If can happen 10,000 miles away.

Once, an earthquake in Chile in South America caused a tidal wave that reached Japan, about 10,000 miles away!

A tidal wave that begins 1,000 miles away is powerful enough to knock down your house if it's less than 50 feet above the beach.

When a strong earthquake shakes the floor of the sea, the rocking and rippling of the water makes a wave on the bottom that rises to the top and travels quickly to shore. When the wave is still out to sea, it may travel at speeds up to 600 miles per hour, about as fast as a jet plane flies. But when the wave approaches shallow water near land, it slows down to 40 miles per hour. However, that doesn't mean it gets less dangerous. At sea a tidal wave, also called a tsunami, may be only 2 feet high. It can pass under a ship without anyone's noticing. But when it gets to shore, it grows to a height of 100 feet or more, about as high as a ten-story building.

Because tsunamis are so huge and they suck up so much water, just before one arrives the ocean looks as if it's getting smaller. It's as though the plug in a bathtub were pulled.

Two hundred years ago in Japan, the sea suddenly seemed to be leaving the harbor. The water ran backward so quickly that fish were stranded on the shore. The townspeople thought a tidal wave was coming, so they ran to the hills above the ocean. Then an earthquake hit and they thought they were wrong, so they went back down to their houses. Soon after, a tidal wave *did* arrive. It destroyed the town and killed most of the people.

On the mountain, you breathe a sigh of relief. The wall of water has smashed down on the beach and now it's gone. You can't wait to get back and head to the dunes. You want to look around and see what's changed.

Is it safe to go back to the beach after a tidal wave has hit?

A. Of course, there's only one tidal wave at a time.

B. Maybe, sometimes there can be two tidal waves in a row.

C. Definitely not, tidal waves travel in groups.

Answer C is right. You definitely should stay away from the beach.

There may be as many as eight tidal waves traveling together. Tsunamis caused by the same earthquake can roar across the ocean 100 miles apart, and the last waves are usually the most destructive. They can be as powerful as an atomic bomb! Just one can wreck an entire town and shave off trees, leaving a forest of stumps. A tsunami can throw a ship from the harbor so that it ends up several miles inland.

What can you do when a tidal wave hits?

It's what you do **before** that counts.

If you've been warned that a wave is due, board up the windows and doors of your house. Secure all loose objects and put your most valuable possessions on the highest floor. Turn off the gas, electricity, and water, then leave immediately for high ground. Stay there until all the waves have hit.

Whatever you do, *don't go down to the beach* to watch the first wave coming! By the time you see it, it'll be too late to get away.

QUAKE

It's early Saturday morning and you're tucked under the covers, reading a book that's too good to put down, the family dog stretched out at your feet. Outside your window, the sun is slowly edging over the trees and the birds are singing a cheerful morning song.

Suddenly the birds fly away in a rush. The wind charges the treetops and a dull rumbling fills the air.

It's only a thunderstorm, you decide. But then the light hanging from the ceiling sways as though you were on a ship. There's moaning and creaking and the furniture starts to rattle. Cracks slither down the walls like snakes. You feel as though you're shivering, but no, it's the whole room that's bouncing up and down!

You're so scared you're sweating and gasping for breath. You can't think. You don't want to believe it, but this is an earthquake!

You run to the window, it's like running uphill. Outside the trees are bumping together like bowling pins. You can barely keep your balance. The house is rocking like a rowboat in a storm. Your desk slides across the room, lamps go flying, books crash from the shelves. You're alone and you're terrified.

What do you do?

A. Crawl under your bed.

B. Stand in the doorway of your room.

C. Kneel under a window with your back to the wall.

D. Climb into a fireplace with your head up the chimney.

The answer is B, stand in the doorway of your room (or any doorway in the middle of your house). That's the safest place to be since it's harder for an earthquake to knock down a doorway than any other part of a building. Besides being strong, doorways cover your head so nothing hanging from the walls or ceiling can fall on you.

If you don't have time to get to a doorway, crawl under your bed or any other strong piece of furniture—the dining room table, or a big solid desk. The furniture will help protect you from anything that is falling. The worst thing about an earthquake is that it knocks down everything around you, from trees to bridges to houses to lamps. What you have to do is to make sure you're in a spot where nothing can hit you.

That means you shouldn't be anywhere near a window. If an earthquake can smash an entire building, just imagine how easily it can break glass.

On the other hand, a wall in the middle of your house has a good chance of making it through an earthquake. Inside walls are the strongest, and the ceiling right above them is the least likely to crumble. Be sure the wall you pick has nothing on it such as bookshelves or pictures to fall on your head. And make sure it doesn't have a chimney. Earthquakes smash chimneys as if their bricks were made of cotton.

But suppose you're not inside your house when an earthquake occurs? You might be walking home from school, thinking about all the homework you have to do. Suddenly you feel the street tremble. . . .

Where do you go?

A. home

B. the nearest building

C. a car

D. none of the above

None of the above is correct.

If you're outside, don't run inside. Get to the most wide-open space you can find, like a park or a meadow, even an empty lot. Whatever you do, stay away from anything that might fall on you.

Don't stand near buildings, trees, or telephone poles. A power line might snap and give you a shock. Don't stay on a bridge or under an overpass—they may fall down.

Suppose you're inside a tall building?

A. Run outside.

B. Get into the elevator and ride up and down.

C. Do exactly what you'd do if you were in a house.

Find a doorway, a heavy piece of furniture, or an inside wall, just as you'd do in a house.

Don't run outside. People who go in and out of buildings during an earthquake are more likely to get hit by falling objects than people who stay in one place. When an earthquake hits, decide on the best thing to do wherever you are and do it.

Don't get into an elevator. The building can shake so much that the cable can snap, or the power can fail and then you'll be stuck.

The earthquake is over very quickly—it doesn't last more than a minute or two. It's suddenly quiet and all the shaking has stopped. You stay where you are for a few minutes just to make sure you're really safe.

What can happen after an earthquake?

A. fires
B. floods
C. more earthquakes
D. all of the above

All of the above can happen.

The first thing you do after an earthquake is check your house for damage. Make sure your parents look around for fires. Fires are caused by gas leaks and electrical problems so if the gas and electricity haven't already been turned off, make sure they are immediately. Then use your nose; you can smell leaking gas. Until you're positive there aren't any gas leaks, don't let anyone smoke or light matches.

You may get down to your basement and discover there's a flood. Earthquakes can break open water pipes. The only way to stop the flood is to turn off the main water line.

And here's something important to keep in mind. You may think the earthquake's over, but it's not. Earthquakes are always followed by other, smaller quakes called after-shocks. There may be one, two, or even more and they may occur a whole day after the original earthquake. An aftershock is caused by the earth's settling into its new position. It's not as strong and powerful as an earthquake, but it can still be dangerous.

What do you do after an earthquake?

A. Drink a big glass of water.
B. Have a bath.
C. Sit down and have a good meal.
D. Explore any buildings that have partly fallen down.
E. None of the above.

None of the above is the correct answer.

After an earthquake, don't use any of the water in your house until you're sure the water supply is safe. Sometimes sewage pipes crack and pollute the water. You might get sick just from brushing your teeth.

Watch out for broken glass. There may be so much of it that it's even in foods and beverages you've left out uncovered. Throw them away.

Before you go out of the house, listen to the radio or television news to make sure it's safe. And whatever you do, if you're out on the street walking around, don't go poking into buildings that have partly fallen down. They may decide to finish falling down—right on top of you!

What causes an earthquake?

A. an explosion in outer space
B. rocks moving underground
C. giants wrestling underground
D. gases exploding beneath the earth

An earthquake is caused by rocks moving underground.

The surface of the earth is made up of about 20 huge plates. The plates are thousands of miles wide and many miles thick. Like turtles with their shells, they carry oceans and continents right on their backs.

All the earth's plates are constantly in motion, although they move very, very slowly, maybe an inch a year. They push each other, trying to slip under or over each other, or to slide past one another. Earthquakes often happen where two plates come together. Along the place where the plates meet, there's a kind of crack in the earth's surface called a fault. The most famous fault in the United States is the San Andreas fault, which runs 600 miles through California and is more than 30 million years old.

An earthquake occurs along a fault when two plates rub together while moving in different directions. The earth shakes and shivers and vibrates like a rubber band that's been snapped. Those vibrations are picked up by a machine called a seismograph, which enables experts to figure out where the earthquake occurred and how strong it was. You measure an earthquake's strength by what scientists have named the Richter Scale. The scale runs from zero to nine, with nine being the most powerful. Sometimes an earthquake occurs so far below the surface, we can hardly feel it on top, but a seismograph tells us it actually happened. Sometimes an earthquake is so strong it has more power than a nuclear explosion. You can feel an earthquake like that 1,200 miles away—the distance from New York to Kansas City—and it can ruin an area the size of Massachusetts. Earthquakes can last five seconds or up to ten minutes and create enough heat to melt any rock.

Is there any way to stop an earthquake from happening?

A. of course
B. only if conditions are right
C. no way

Earthquakes cannot be prevented. Scientists can't even predict when they'll happen. However, some experts think that one day we'll be able to do both. They believe that by measuring the gases that come out of the earth, we'll be able to predict earthquakes accurately. We'll prevent them by pumping a lot of water into wells near the places earthquakes start, then draining that water out. All over the world, scientists are experimenting on ways to predict and prevent earthquakes. That's very important work, since there are more than 1 million earthquakes a year! Of course, we don't hear about most of them because they happen under the sea.

Even if they can't predict and prevent earthquakes, scientists do have a good idea *where* they'll happen. So if you're not sure whether you live in earthquake country, you can easily find out. Call the National Weather Service or go to your library and check the latest earthquake map.

At some time or another, earthquakes have hit almost every part of the United States, but more have struck California and Nevada than anywhere else. Most scientists believe the next great American earthquake will happen somewhere in California, but a strong one may strike the east coast, too.

You're a little worried now because you live in a place an earthquake has hit and may hit again. You look around your house, and it still seems solid and strong. But you wonder. . . .

Is there anything you can do to get ready for an earthquake?
A. Learn how to turn off the gas, electricity, and water.
B. Know how to use a fire extinguisher.
C. Keep emergency supplies ready.
D. All of the above.

You can't stop the earthquake from happening, but if you know one might hit, you can certainly get ready for it by doing all of the above.

Learn where to go in your house to turn off the gas, electricity, and water. You may want your parents to nail or bolt down the stove or furnace and anything else that runs on gas. That way nothing can slide across the floor and break open gas lines. An open gas line can start a fire.

Always keep a fire extinguisher nearby and know how to use it. Make sure you have emergency supplies on hand: canned food, bottled water, a battery-operated radio, blankets, and a flashlight.

And decide *now* exactly where you're going to go in your house if an earthquake hits. Don't wait until one happens or it may be too late.

It's even possible to find out if a house is strong enough to survive a big earthquake. Scientists know exactly how to make sure it will, and many houses in earthquake country are built according to their advice. One of the things earthquake experts advise is to try not to build a house on the side of mountain.

Why shouldn't you build a house on the side of a mountain?

A. It can slide off.

B. The mountain can split in two.

C. There might be a landslide or an avalanche.

Since an earthquake makes everything shiver and shake, if there are loose rocks or snow or dirt on a mountain, they may all come tumbling down. When that happens, there's a landslide or an avalanche.

In 1970, a town built on the side of a mountain in Peru just disappeared one day. First there was an earthquake. The earthquake caused an avalanche and after that a landslide. The side of the mountain slid down and covered the town completely. There were rocks as big as houses and tons and tons of dirt. Clouds of red dust hung over the mountainside and people could see these clouds for miles and miles.

You're feeling very lucky. Nothing really terrible happened to you. When you go out on the street, it looks almost normal. If you didn't know there'd been an earthquake, you might not be able to tell.

But some earthquakes can be very destructive. Once in a while, a big earthquake hits and people die and houses are destroyed.

What happens in the worst earthquakes?

A. Highways crack open.

B. Railroad tracks tear apart.

C. Bridges crash down.

D. Dams burst open.

E. Streets cave in.

F. Forests fall down.

G. All of the above.

Earthquakes can be so destructive that all of the above can happen—and more! Terrible fires can start. In 1906, San Francisco, California, had an earthquake, and the fire it started burned for three days. The whole city was almost destroyed.

Tall buildings can fall down, and people can get buried alive. In Europe in 1977, Rumania had an earthquake. An apartment building fell down on a retired schoolteacher, and it took eight days for rescuers to save her. When at last they found her, they discovered that all that had happened to her was that she had a broken leg!

That woman was very lucky. The year before in China, an earthquake killed 655,000 people—that's equal to the population of Atlanta, Georgia.

So the earthquake that hit your house was a lot less powerful—most earthquakes aren't strong enough to be *that* destructive. And at least only one happened that day.

How many earthquakes can happen in a day?

A. just 1

B. 2

C. 3

D. 10

E. 25

F. 10,000

In 1966 in Japan, one town had 10,000 earthquakes in a single day! Of course, most of the earthquakes were so small that only a seismograph sensed them.

Still, all the townspeople felt enough trembling from these quakes to become nervous. During that year, the same town had 450,000 earthquakes—on some days, one every two minutes! The earth never seemed to stop its shaking. Buildings began to crack. People became so scared they couldn't sleep. Every night they turned off the utilities, left their houses, and camped out in the fields. That way, they thought, nothing could fall on them.

Scientists call such a rapid succession of earthquakes an earthquake swarm. Did many people get hurt because of it? Luckily, not a single one was injured.

SHIPWRECK

You can hardly believe it. Everywhere you look, there is nothing but water. The endless sky and the endless sea are almost the same color. It's been five days since you last walked on land, but you're so used to the rolling waves now that the deck of the sailboat feels like the sidewalk. What a great vacation: you and your family out on a big sailboat, fishing and swimming, taking it easy.

Up until now, the weather's been perfect. But just before lunchtime, after your swim, you notice a dark cloud moving quickly in the distance. "We're going to get rain," your mother announces, but nobody gives it a second thought.

Then the day becomes grayer and grayer. The waves begin to toss and spit. Lightning from nowhere dives into the water and the wind turns angry and cold. Everyone rushes into the boat's cabin when the storm finally hits.

Now you look outside and the afternoon seems like midnight. The waves are tall enough to block out the sky. The boat rocks so fast it's like a seesaw gone crazy as it's slammed down by one wave, then thrown up by another. You're feeling so sick you don't even want to breathe.

Objects fly off the table and smash against the walls. You're pushed and pulled and tossed and turned. Your heart beats against your chest just like the waves against the boat. No one, not even your parents, hears you screaming because the storm is so loud.

Suddenly there's a roar, and a wave like a hammer pounds on the deck. There's a crack and a crash and water pours into the cabin as if it were a bathtub. You're slipping and sliding, you can barely stand up! The cabin's filling with water, climbing up to your knees. You're in real danger. You've got to save yourself.

What's the first thing you do?

A. Put on your life jacket.

B. Radio the Coast Guard.

C. Go to the bathroom.

D. Get your life raft ready to be launched.

You should already have your life jacket on, since experts feel it should be worn all the time. But if you don't, the first thing you should do is put on your life jacket. Forget about everything else until you do that. And make sure everyone on the boat is wearing one, too. You don't know how fast your boat is sinking, and the waves are all around you. There's water everywhere. Maybe the life raft can't be launched in such a storm. But once your life jacket's on, at least you know you'll stay afloat if you have to get into the water. It will also help keep you a little warmer.

Now you think about what else to do. You can see the boat getting lower in the water. Each time a wave hits it, it shakes like a trampoline. Your father runs to the radio. He's calling the Coast Guard. He's got to tell them where you are. They'll send out a ship or a helicopter to try to rescue you. ALWAYS CALL THE COAST GUARD IF YOU HAVE TIME BEFORE YOUR BOAT SINKS.

You look around for your mother. She's loading up the life raft and wants you to help. Suddenly you get going. You grab a bottle of water from the cabin and wade to the deck. First it's like walking uphill, then it's like sliding downhill. The waves just won't let the boat alone. You think it's time to launch the life raft. Anyplace seems safer than a tilting boat.

When is it time to launch the life raft?
A. whenever you're ready
B. when you're sure the boat is sinking
C. after you've gotten your favorite things

Forget about your favorite things and forget about being ready. If you're sure the boat is sinking, you have to launch your life raft, *no matter what*. But you should never launch your life raft unless the boat is actually sinking. Some boats go under very quickly and all you have time to do is put on your life jacket and get into your life raft. One family's boat sank in just 60 seconds when killer whales attacked it and tore out its bottom. They didn't even have time to call the Coast Guard! But usually a boat sinks a lot more slowly; it might not go under for a long time or it might not go under at all. So stay with the

63

boat for as long as you can—it's safer than a raft in the middle of the ocean.

If you have to use your raft, it should be loaded with supplies. That's what your family's doing right now. Everyone's racing back and forth between the cabin and the deck, carrying all the things you'll need. The raft should have been loaded before you left shore, but no one thought anything like this would happen. Next time, you think, you'll be more prepared.

You're feeling calmer now since there's too much to do to be scared. But you know the water in the boat is rising. You practically have to swim to get anywhere. Suddenly a huge wave, a monster, appears on the side. There's another wave right in front. As if it's just been punched, the boat flips over. Everyone scrambles to the other side.

The boat is really sinking now. It's time to get into the rubber raft.

You're wet and you're cold, and you're tired and you're frightened. From the raft you watch your sailboat sinking in front of you. No one can look at anything else. At last it disappears into the water. Now it's your family and the raft and the sea. You've got just a little water; you've got just a little food; you've got just enough room for all of you to fit. The storm is nearly over. A bit of sun lights the sky. You see unknown objects floating around you.

Do you know what those objects are?

A. garbage from shore

B. dead fish and birds

C. parts of your boat

They're probably parts of your boat. When a boat sinks, debris usually comes to the surface. Debris is anything on the boat that is loose and can float—it might be wood or supplies from the cabin. Debris is the reason that experts tell you never to leave the spot where your boat sinks. Wait and see if any debris you can use in your raft rises to the surface.

You should stay where you are anyway, if you've radioed the Coast Guard. Since you've told them your location, that's where they'll be sending a rescue ship.

From the raft, you look carefully at the debris. Something heavy slams into the side. When you reach over to pull it up, a wave hits you in the face. You grab it anyway, salt water coating your throat. It's your father's fishing equipment! Now you'll be able to fish for food if you have to. Everyone keeps eyes glued to the ocean. There are plastic water bottles floating around, too! Now you'll have more to drink. You'll also be able to bail the raft out when waves spill over the sides of the raft, filling it up with water.

Finally night falls and the sea is almost calm. Your father puts up a canopy. A canopy is like a little tent, and every life raft has one. It fits neatly around the inside of the raft and gives protection from the wind, the rain, and the waves. During the day, it keeps you from getting sunburned. Without a canopy, you can die of exposure if you have to sit directly in the cold or in the sun.

The night passes slowly. The only sound is the water lapping at the sides of the raft. In the morning, you wake up and realize you've drifted away from the spot your boat sank. Now nobody's sure what to do. Nobody knows if the Coast Guard will find you.

How are you going to get rescued?

A. Pray.

B. Put a message in a bottle and hope it gets to shore.

C. Keep watch and signal if you see something.

The correct answer is C.

Everyone has to take turns being a lookout—there can't be any time of day or night when someone isn't keeping watch, when someone isn't ready to signal. Boats can sail close to you at any hour, but if you don't see them first, they might pass right by you. The ocean is so big and the raft is so small, it's very hard to see. You might spot a big ship two and a half miles away—that's how far you can sometimes see from your raft on a clear day—but that ship won't see you unless you signal. Be prepared to signal any way you can. If you have them, use flares or a flashlight. In the daytime, wave the brightest clothing you have in the air. If you have a mirror, let the sun reflect off it. That makes a very bright light.

But what if you're shipwrecked for days and no ship comes by?

If you have a compass and you know how to use it, try to head for shore. If there's no compass aboard but someone has a watch, you can still figure out which way you're going. Wait for a sunny day. Lie the watch flat in your palm, pointing the hour hand at the sun. South will be halfway between the hour hand and 12:00. Once you know where south is, you know where north and east and west are too.

If you're too far from land to make it there in a few days, see if you can reach what's called a shipping lane, where most boats travel in the ocean. Any good chart will show you where to find one.

So there you are in the raft, with nothing but water and sky all around you. You can hardly remember what your sailboat looked like. The sea is so calm, it's hard to believe there was a storm just last night. The morning sun makes you feel warm and cozy. For a minute, you think being shipwrecked is fun. After all, you don't have to go to school, you'll end up with a pretty nice tan, you'll lose a little weight, and you might even learn to swim better.

Is being shipwrecked fun?

A. absolutely not

B. sure

C. depends

Being shipwrecked is awful. That's what everyone who's been through it has said. You may not feel uncomfortable yet, but soon you'll be uncomfortable all the time. You'll get wet and you'll get cold. You'll try drying off in the sun but then you'll get hot and sometimes even burned. The only way to cool off is to dump some sea water over yourself, but then you'll be wet all over again. After a few days of that, you'll break out in blisters, little bits of your skin will puff up and break open. When salt water gets inside them, they'll sting. Because they're wet all the time, your clothes will start to fall apart so you'll be even colder at night and hotter in the day. Your skin will get even more irritated.

Right now, the sea is calm. But at any hour it can rise again. There's the constant noise of the waves and the wind. Sometimes you'll get seasick. You'll be depressed and tired, frightened and cranky. You'll begin to imagine things and often lose your temper. All you'll think about is food and water—even if you have some, you'll worry about where you're going to get more. Your mouth will feel constantly dry. Your knees and ankles and wrists will get stiff. All the bones in your body will begin to ache—it will even hurt to sit.

So forget about having fun when you're shipwrecked. You won't want to do it any longer than you have to. By night you'll dream about rescue and eating your favorite dessert. By day you'll stare at the sea, desperate to get back to land. You'll wonder how long you've been floating around. You'll wonder how much longer you'll have to. And you'll try not to think about the REALLY BIG question.

How long can you stay alive if you're shipwrecked?

A. just a few days
B. up to two weeks
C. no more than a month
D. none of the above

How long you stay alive depends on how much food and water you've started out with and how much you can find while you wait to be rescued. So the answer is D, none of the above.

People who are shipwrecked and don't know what to do can die within days. If the temperature outside is around 50 degrees, you can live for about ten days without water. But if it's hot, around 80 degrees, you might not live more than three days. You need to drink at least a pint of water a day—that's one large glass—to survive in hot weather. If you drink less—just a cup, for example—you might not live longer than ten days. If you have water but no food, you'll last longer than if you have food but no water: people with water but no food have lived for up to a month! If you have plenty of food but not much water, you should eat very little. Food can make you thirsty, and you also need water to digest it.

So there you are on the raft, floating and floating. You guess there's enough food and water for about five days. But what if you're shipwrecked longer?

How do you get food and water when you run out of supplies on a life raft in the middle of the ocean?

A. Catch fish and suck their bones.

B. Drink the blood of turtles.

C. Cut open birds' stomachs and eat what's in them.

D. Drink rainwater.

E. All of the above.

As awful as it sounds, you should do all of the above.

When you run out of supplies and you're shipwrecked, you have to depend on the sea and the sky to keep alive. You catch food from the sea and rain from the sky. There'll be plenty of fish all around you. Some will even bump their heads on the bottom of your raft. Flying fish will jump so high out of the water they'll often land in the seat right next to you. You may think now you could never kill a fish, but when you get hungry enough, you will. To make sure fish don't jump right out of the raft and back into the water, take two of your fingers and press one on each of a fish's eyes. The fish will become paralyzed.

You'll be able to catch fish with hooks and a line, your father's fishing equipment you found in the sailboat's debris. But if you lose your line, you can use your shoelaces! And if you have no hooks, use your imagination—you'll find something else that will do. One couple was shipwrecked for 118 days, that's almost four months, when their boat was sunk by a whale. They didn't have fishing hooks so they used open safety pins!

Sometimes there are so many fish right around your raft that you can catch one with your hands if you're quick enough. One family got so good at fishing this way, they actually caught small *sharks* with their bare hands!

After you kill a fish, cut what you don't eat right away into little pieces. Lay them in the sun to dry. Make sure the pieces don't get wet or they'll rot. You don't have to worry about having insects landing on them—there aren't any out in the middle of the ocean! Drying out pieces prevents spoilage. Eating spoiled fish can really make you sick.

Don't throw the fish bones away: pick them clean, then break open the spine. Drink and suck what you can from the little bones in the spine—there's water and protein in them. You should also eat the eyes of the fish, its liver, its brain, and its pancreas. These organs all contain vitamin C, which you'll need. You probably think that this sounds so disgusting that you'd never do it, but when you're starving on the raft and are worried about scurvy, you'll eat them. Scurvy is a disease you can get when you don't have enough vitamin C. Your gums get soft, your teeth loosen, and your skin bruises very easily.

Fish are not the only food in the sea. Turtles will also swim under your raft. If you feel you could never eat a turtle, wait till you've been shipwrecked for a few days.

You have to be quick to catch a turtle, though. Pick it up and throw it on its back in the bottom of the raft. Watch out that you don't get bitten—yes, turtles bite. To kill it, cut its throat and then drink the blood. No matter how nauseated the idea makes you, you have to drink the blood—it's full of vitamins and water.

Turtle meat tastes good. Do the same thing with it that you do with fish: Cut the meat up in little pieces and let it dry out in the sun thoroughly. That way it will last much longer. If you catch a female turtle, she may be full of eggs. Eat them; they're good for you and you'll probably like them.

Aside from making a good meal, turtles can be useful in another way. One couple tied ropes around some and let them pull their raft through the waves!

Birds will also come near the raft, in fact, they'll probably land on it. Birds that live so far away from shore aren't afraid of people. If you catch one, kill it and cut open its stomach right away. If it's just been fishing, its stomach will be full of fresh fish that are still undigested. Eat them. You'll be so hungry you won't care where the fish came from.

But it's even more important to get fresh water than to get food. You might have a desalinization kit on your raft. Every life raft should have one. A desalinization kit lets you take the salt out of saltwater so you can drink it. If you don't have one on board, you'll have to depend on the weather. The only other way to get fresh water in the middle of the ocean is to catch some when it rains. Use the canopy of your raft to collect rainwater. When it first starts to rain, let the drops wash the salt from the waves off the canopy. If it's warm enough, you can let the rain wash you off, too. When you think it's washed enough, put your freshwater bottles at the bottom of the canopy and catch the rain as it runs off. When a bottle fills up, don't forget to put the cap on and tie the bottle to the raft. That way you won't lose any water if a wave washes over the raft.

If it gets very cold outside, put some sea water in a bottle and see if it will freeze. If it does, all the salt will stay in the middle. You'll be able to see it—it looks like slush. Just dig it out with your hands and when the rest of the iced water melts, you can drink it. If you're floating near icebergs, drink the water from any part of the icebergs you can find. The water in icebergs is fresh.

Keep in mind that if you're short on water, you should move around as little as possible. The less active you are, the less water you'll need. If you've gone a long time without water and then you get some, drink it slowly at first, in small sips. Drinking it quickly can make you feel sick. If it's hot, wet your clothes with sea water and sit in the shade of the canopy in a breeze. You'll sweat less and won't need as much water.

Days have passed now. You're incredibly thirsty. All of your water is gone. You do nothing but watch the sky for dark clouds so you'll know when the rains will come. Then you'll be able to drink your fill. You're not sure you can wait for the rain. After all, there's water all around you.

Can't you just drink from the sea?

A. of course

B. definitely not

C. just a little, and only if you mix it with fresh water

DEFINITELY NOT, drinking saltwater can kill you! It makes you even more thirsty than you were before. It makes you feel sick. But worst of all, it can make you go crazy.

Saltwater affects your brain. You begin to see things that aren't there; you hear voices even though no one is talking. People who drink saltwater sometimes dive off the life raft and drown.

You're hungry, you're hot, and you're bored. Days have passed, even weeks. The raft is still floating, floating. You bail it out whenever it gets full of water. You spend your time hiding from the sun, avoiding the wind. You're always crouched under your canopy trying to stay fit by doing some muscle-stretching exercises. Suddenly things seem a little bit different. There's a strange new feel to the air. Is that land in the distance? You can't be sure.

How can you tell if you're getting close to land even though you can't see it?

A. The water fades to a lighter color.
B. More birds than ever are flying overhead, all in the same direction.
C. The smell of the air is less like the smell of the sea.
D. Seaweed is floating on the surface.
E. All of the above.

All of the above are signs that land is near.

How do you land on the beach?

A. Jump into the water and swim to shore.
B. Catch a really big wave and ride it in.
C. Wait for the smallest waves and paddle in.

Always wait for the water to be as calm as it can get. The bigger the waves are, the more chance there is that your raft will overturn or crash against the rocks. Never jump out of the raft and think you can swim to shore. It's always safer in your boat than it is in the water.

THE EMPTY CANTEEN

You thought the desert would be white sand and dunes, but here it is, mostly rocks and dirt and mountains and canyons. Some of it's red and some of it's brown, some of it's tan, and some is even purple—it's the most beautiful place you've ever seen.

You've been hiking since early this morning and now your group is taking a rest. There's a hill in the distance with a nice view so you decide to walk over by yourself.

At the top when you look around, it's like the earth and the sky exist just for you. It must be miles to any road. Ahead the flat land is glowing in the sunlight. The air seems to break into waves. So much heat is rising from the ground, everything looks as if it's trembling. You're hot and thirsty, so you drink from your canteen. It's nearly empty.

You start heading back to your group. You're sure the spot where they're resting is just to the left, but everything looks the same. You walk and walk—they must be over there. Rocks crumble under your boots; dust flies into your mouth. What you'd give for a nice cool swim!

Now the sun is so hot you feel as though you're cooking: You could be a steak on a grill that's getting well done. When you try to wet your lips, all you taste is sweat and sand. You're getting scared.

Where can your group have gone? You don't see them anywhere. When you shout as loudly as you can, no one answers.

Could you be lost?

You're so hot you could faint. The sun is rising higher; the sky is pale from the heat; the earth looks dead and dry.

What are you going to do now?

A. Find shade.

B. Relax and get a great tan.

C. Dig for water.

D. Shout some more.

If you're lost in the desert and it's almost the middle of the day, you have to get out of the sun. *Find shade.* Even in the shade the temperature might reach 120 degrees! The heat you feel isn't only from the sun's rays. Heat also comes up from the ground when the sun reflects off the sand. The ground itself can be 200 degrees. That's hot enough to burn your feet right through your sneakers! Luckily, you're wearing your hiking boots.

When the sun's out, it's just too hot to be good for you. Being in the desert isn't like being at the beach, and you know how sunburned you can get there. Don't take your shirt off no matter how hot you get. If you have some in your supplies, use plenty of suntan lotion and apply petroleum jelly to your lips. Don't walk around between 10:00 A.M. and 4:00 P.M.—that's when it's hottest. Wear a hat— it will help keep you cool—and protect your eyes by wearing sunglasses. Rest a lot.

You're scared and you're lonely but you have to find shade. You know you should stay as close as possible to where you are now, since your group will start searching for you in the last place you were seen. Ahead you see a funny-shaped boulder. It has a bump that makes a nice patch of shade underneath. Maybe that would be a good place to sit.

There's one problem with sitting under that boulder. *Can you guess what it is?*

A. It's hotter under boulders.
B. You're harder to see.
C. A rock could fall on your head.

You're harder to see. The biggest mistake lost people make is staying out of sight. Rescue teams in helicopters and airplanes will be searching for you. You want to make it easy for them to spot you. It's OK to sit under that boulder. But make some sign that can be seen from far away. Use different-colored stones to make a big *X* on the ground. Write *HELP* in the sand with the toe of your shoe. Searchers will come looking in jeeps, on horseback, and on foot, too. If you see anyone, wave your arms, jump up and down, and do whatever you can think of to attract attention. But while you're waiting, stay calm. Kids lost in the desert are almost always found within 24 hours.

You write *HELP* and draw a huge arrow in the sand with a sharp rock. Then you settle down under the boulder. It doesn't feel that much cooler in the shade. But at least you know the shade won't cause heat stroke, dry you out, give you cramps. The sun could do all of that to you.

If you hadn't found the boulder and you couldn't see any shade in the distance, how could you have made shade for yourself?
A. by finding rocks and picking them up
B. by digging a hole
C. all of the above
D. none of the above

In some deserts, there are lots of small rocks you can easily gather and pile up. When you finish, there will be some shade on one side of the pile. Be careful not to put your hands under the rocks when you lift them—a snake or a spider might be sleeping there to stay cool. A good rule is not to put your hands or feet anywhere you can't see.

If you can't find any rocks, dig a hole in the sand and cover yourself up—even that's better than having the rays of the sun on your body.

Under the boulder, you feel as though you've been lost for days. The heat is making you very sleepy, and you decide you might as well take a nap. Out you stretch. When you wake up, all you can think of is how thirsty you are. You finish every drop of water in your canteen but still your mouth is dry. The sun is getting lower. You decide it's safe to come out of the shade. You're not going to go far, but you need to look for water.

How much water do you think you should drink each day you're in the desert?

A. a glass

B. a quart

C. a gallon

In the desert, you need to drink a gallon of water a day—that's about eight tall glasses. If you've got a gallon of water to drink, you can walk close to 15 miles a day. How much food do you need each day? Surprisingly, you can go for many days without eating, as long as you have water.

What do you do to find water?

A. Go to the top of a hill.

B. Start digging.

C. Look for beach umbrellas.

D. None of the above.

It's very hard to find water in the desert, but if you're near a hill, it can be worth climbing up to take a look. Just keep in mind that walking in the desert heat uses up your body's water. Even though you don't feel wet, you're sweating all the time. Don't go far and don't do much. That's one reason you shouldn't start digging. You're likely to sweat out more water than you'll find. Another reason is that digging isn't likely to get you water anyway.

Here's what to do: Go to the highest place you can find close by. If there's a hill or a tree, climb it because the higher you are, the more you'll see. There may just be water right near you. Sometimes you can spot its reflection in the sunlight. It might have collected in little potholes along rocky hills. Or there might be a large water hole, like a pond, not too far away. Remember, though—

it's hard to figure out how far away things are in the desert. That may have been why you got lost. The clear air, the sunlight, and the changing shadows all play tricks on your eyes. What looks close might still be a long way off.

You also have to watch out for mirages. That's when a lake dries out and fills with hot air. The empty lake hole reflects the blue sky as though it were a mirror and you can be fooled into thinking water is there.

If you can't spot any water, look for anything green—a clump of trees, a group of bushes. A green place in the desert is called an oasis, and it couldn't be green if water weren't nearby.

There's a hill right near your boulder. It doesn't look as though it'll be that hard to climb. But right near the top, the dirt keeps slipping under your feet. You slide a little way down, but you're determined to make it. At last you're there. *How lucky can you be?* There's a water hole just down past the hill. You're sure it's nearby; you're sure it's not a mirage.

In a few minutes, you get there. It's hard to believe there's all that water in front of you. You want to throw yourself in it; you want to gulp it all down. But first you look around.

Is the surface of the water very still?

Is there a bad smell in the air?

Are there no signs that animals have been drinking there?

When you take a sip, does it taste funny in your mouth?

Stop! Don't drink it! THE WATER'S POISON!

Once in a great while in the desert, a poison called arsenic soaks into the water hole. Also, desert water can sometimes be very salty. If it is, don't drink it. Saltwater isn't good for you.

How can you tell if it's safe to drink water?

A. Tadpoles are swimming around in it.
B. Bugs are jumping in and out of it.
C. There's green, slimy stuff called algae on the surface.
D. Worms and spiders are floating in it.
E. There are paw prints in the sand.
F. There's a fresh smell in the air.
G. All of the above.

All of the above are signs of drinkable water.

All of the above? Yes. No matter how disgusting tadpoles and spiders, worms and algae look, the fact that they're living in the water means it's safe to drink. You can take a handkerchief or shirt or anything cotton and filter the water through it. The bugs and dirt will stay on the cotton and you'll have pure water to drink.

But there's no water you can drink right now.

Are there any other ways to find water in the desert?

A. Look for a cave.
B. Watch for animals.
C. Drink the early morning dew.
D. Chop up a cactus.
E. All of the above.

You already know it's hard to find water in the desert, but every one of the ways listed above have helped some lucky people find it.

Don't go out of your way to look for caves, but if one's

in sight nearby, it just might have a pool of water inside it. Of course, caves are also shady and cool, so you'll sweat less and need less to drink if you stay in one. But you have to be careful. Snakes may have found this cave before you. And don't forget, if you go in, leave some sign outside that can be seen from a helicopter.

Some people say that if by some chance you spot an animal in the desert it might be heading for water. Stay out of its way and don't go far, but notice where it goes. There just may be a water hole within walking distance. Desert animals can go without water longer than other animals but they always know where it is. You may not see wildlife during the day, but as the sun is setting, animals will certainly come out. Depending on which kind of desert you're in, you may spot deer or bobcats, burros or rabbits, coyotes or foxes, bighorn sheep or raccoons. There may even be skunks and wild horses.

In the winter, you may find water in the early morning. It's then that the desert has dew—water that forms from the cool air at night. Take your shirt or anything made of cotton and wipe the dew off plants, bushes, cacti, even rocks. Squeeze the water into your mouth. People lost in the desert have survived until they could find a water hole by drinking dew.

The most difficult way to get water in the desert is by chopping up a cactus. Most experts think you shouldn't even try. They say it's so hard to cut open a cactus that you actually sweat out more water doing it than you get to drink. Cacti can also be dangerous since their needles are as sharp as knives. Some needles grow up from the ground and it's hard to see them. You can be a few feet away from the cactus itself and still step on one of those needles. It can rip right through your shoe and into your foot.

But some people say they survived in the desert by drinking the water of cacti. This must have been in the spring, since by summer most of the water in a cactus has been used up. Those who survived cut off parts of small cacti and peeled off the skin. By sucking on the pieces, they got a little water. Large cacti such as the saguaro have a few drops more. The saguaro is like a cactus tree and it's the kind you most often see in cowboy movies. You chop off its top and dig out the middle, which is mushy, like the inside of a peach. Mash it and stir it, then squeeze out the water. It's bitter but it's safe to drink.

So there you are standing by a poisoned water hole with an empty canteen. The sun is getting lower. The endless wind blows sand in your face. You've just got to get water. You're feeling weaker by the minute. You're not sure you can go on. Suddenly you hear thunder and see huge dark clouds approaching. Lightning tears them open and out pours rain! You have to do something.

Do you:

A. run for cover so you don't get wet?
B. open the umbrella you were carrying just in case?
C. stay out and get drenched?

Stay out in the rain and get drenched. Your wet clothes will keep you cool for more than an hour, even after the hot sun comes out again. And don't forget to lean back and open your mouth—when the rain pours in, you'll have a good long drink.

Drink as much water as you want. In fact, drink *more* water than you want. Think of your stomach as a big storage tank. You may not need it now, but your body will use it up later. If you have a bottle or a bucket or your canteen, be sure to open it up and catch as much rainwater as you can. Remember, whenever you're thirsty, take a drink. Never ration it. Rationing water means you're saving it: Although you feel thirsty, you drink only a few drops at a time because you want your water to last for days. Rationing is dangerous. Because of it, people die in the desert even though their canteens are nearly full.

Do you know how lucky you are that it rained? There are some deserts in the world where it doesn't rain for *years*. Death Valley, in the United States, gets less than 2 inches a year. On the other hand, parts of Hawaii have rains of 400 inches a year! It's so hot in some deserts that even when it rains, the ground never gets wet; the raindrops burn up in the air before they reach the land. Scientists call any part of the world that gets less than 10 inches of rain a year a desert.

But you *were* lucky, and it rained. You're cooler now and at last you're not thirsty. But there's something the rain does that you have to watch out for.

Can you

A. get caught in a flood?
B. catch pneumonia from getting drenched?
C. get blown over by the high winds?

You can get caught in a flood.

Floods? In the desert? It doesn't make sense, but it's true. Desert rains, especially summer storms, can sometimes cause flash floods. A flash flood happens very quickly and doesn't last too long, which is good, because it can be very frightening.

When it rains in the desert, it really pours. The raindrops can be as big as hailstones, and at first they kick a lot of dust into the air. The land is so dry, it can't soak up the water so most of it stays on top of the ground. It starts to run very fast down old streambeds, over low ground, and through long cuts in the earth. As it runs, it gets very deep—in a big storm, up to 20 feet deep! A flash flood is also very strong, snapping trees in half, pulling bushes out by their roots. Some hikers once watched a flash flood smash apart their car!

Sometimes it takes an hour for the flood to begin. The rain has stopped, the sun is out, the sky is clear, and you're hot all over again. Nothing even looks wet anymore. Suddenly the earth shivers, as if an earthquake were beginning. There's a crack and a roar and a wall of water rushes right at you. But it doesn't look like water since it's not blue or green. It's the color of the desert sand—red or brown—and it's so thick with that sand, that it's a little like soup. Because of flash floods, you should never sleep overnight in old streambeds or on low ground.

After the rain, there's a fresh smell to the desert. It's suddenly easy to find water. You sit down on a rock to enjoy the cool air and watch the sun sinking in the distance. The edge of the sky is purple and orange and red and blue—almost like a rainbow. Suddenly you hear a faint scraping from nearby. You decide to ignore it, then it happens again.

Something inside you tells you not to move. Some instinct says you might be in danger. You certainly don't want whatever it is to crawl up your leg or creep under your clothes. After all, it could be a scorpion; it could be a black widow spider; it could be a Gila monster; it could be a rattlesnake.

You stay very still. You're afraid even to breathe. You don't move your hands and legs even a little bit.

At last it goes away. You can relax. What could it have been? An insect? A lizard? A snake? It might have been any of those things and some of them are poisonous! On the other hand, it might have been a bird or a mouse. In any case, most desert creatures won't bother you unless you bother them. Some experts say a Gila monster won't bite you unless you *force* your fingers into its mouth!

Still, you can't help wondering.

Suppose you do come across a rattlesnake? What should you do?

A. Throw a big rock at it.

B. Jump up and down and stamp on the ground.

C. Run as fast as you can as far as you can without stopping.

D. Walk around it—way around it.

E. Stay very, very still.

F. Pick it up by its rattle and throw it hard against the ground.

G. None of the above.

Usually the best way to deal with a rattlesnake, if you see it, is to walk around it so it can't bite you just by stretching out. But you're likely to walk past a rattlesnake without even seeing it. A rattlesnake is very hard to spot because the color of its skin matches the colors of the sand. Scientists call that camouflage. And most rattlesnakes are very lazy—unless you really scare them, they won't attack you.

It's very rare for anyone to get bitten or stung by a poisonous creature in the desert. The best way to avoid a problem is just to watch where you're going. If desert creatures come out during the day, they're looking for shade. So you should never stick your hand into anything or under anything unless you're sure there's nothing there.

And don't worry: When you're out there in the desert, walking around in the baking sun or lying down in the shade to get some sleep, a mosquito is much more likely to bite you than a rattlesnake, a Gila monster, a scorpion, or a spider. There are mosquitoes in the desert and you're a tasty meal. You'll be scratching away, thinking about the blisters on your feet and the small bugs called gnats that are attacking your eyes. There'll be velvet ants that bite crawling right near you, and stinging red wasps buzzing around your head. In some deserts, the wind blows constantly—the wind that can make sand dunes in some deserts more than 600 feet high, as tall as a 50-story building!

If the wind is strong enough, what else can it do?
A. Knock you over.
B. Cause a duststorm or sandstorm.
C. Make all the rattlesnakes in the desert come out.

A 50-mile-an-hour wind can cause a sandstorm or a

duststorm. Sand will get into your food, your water, your clothes, your eyes. Dust will be everywhere: You won't be able to see the sun. A sandstorm can make a moving wall of dust 5,000 feet high—that's almost a mile into the sky! And if a sandstorm and a rainstorm hit at the same time, you have a mudstorm!

Night is falling now, and you can hear all sorts of strange noises. Screech owls are hooting, toads are croaking, bats are squeaking their way through the air. But that's not what's bothering you. You can't figure out why you're shivering.

A. Is it cold?

B. Are you getting sick?

C. Are you just scared?

Deserts are actually cold at night, so if you're shivering, it's probably because the temperature has dropped. It can be 80 degrees warmer during the day than at night: The temperature can actually fall below freezing. People have sometimes gotten frostbite in the desert!

Hard though it is to believe, some deserts are cold all the time—they can be covered with snow and ice the whole year round. Scientists call such deserts cold deserts. One-sixth of the world is cold desert! But it wasn't always this way. Twenty million years ago, Antarctica was so warm it was almost like a jungle. Hot deserts weren't always hot either. The Painted Desert in California used to have pine trees and ferns—and dinosaurs! Seventy million years ago, the Sahara (the world's largest desert) was completely covered by a sea.

There may be even more, different deserts millions of

years from now.

If you're lost in a desert where it gets cold at night, you have to find shelter. Look for a clump of trees or a ledge under which you can sleep. There'll be less wind there to bother you. You can also pile up stones all around you to cut down on the wind. You might want to lie down on a large, flat rock because it could still be warm from the daytime sun. If you have to sleep on the sand, dig it up first with the heel of your boot or a rock. Desert sand is crunchy and hard, unlike the sand at the beach, so you'll want to soften it up.

It might be so cold that you have to build a fire. If there's no firewood around, burn dead cacti plants or bushes. In the morning, make sure the fire is completely out. The desert wind can be strong enough to start a blaze from a leftover spark.

If you're hiking in a desert that gets cold at night, you should always bring some wool clothing and a jacket with you. During the day when it's warm, wear loose, light-colored cotton clothes—they're cooler. At night, wear wool—it's warmer. The hat that keeps the sun off your head by day at night will keep your body heat in.

You fold your arms around you and stare into the night. Suddenly you hear something—a buzzing in the air. Searchlights are sweeping the desert. It's a helicopter! You run into the glare and wave your arms until the rescue team sees you. "Just stay put," a voice calls. "We'll have you right out of here."

You're safe! You've never felt so happy. You know you shouldn't have wandered off by yourself, you know you're lucky you're alive. But all you can think of now that you know you're going to be rescued is drinking the longest, tallest lemonade of your life.